THE ENDANGERED SPECIES COOKBOOK

B.R. "Buck" Peterson

Illustrations by J. Angus "Sourdough" McLean

TEN SPEED PRESS
Berkeley, California

1🕊

TEN SPEED PRESS
P.O. Box 7123
Berkeley, California 94707

Cover design by Fifth Street Design
Text design by Faith and Folly
Illustrations by J. Angus "Sourdough" McLean

Library of Congress Cataloging in Publication Data

Peterson, B. R.
    The endangered species cookbook / B. R. "Buck" Peterson
      p. cm.
    ISBN 0-89815-556-8 :
    1. Cookery—Humor. 2. Endangered species—Humor. I. Title.
PN6231.C624P39   1993
818'.5407—dc20   93-32497
                                                         CIP

Printed in the United States of America

1 2 3 4 5 — 97 96 95 94 93

This book is dedicated to my friend Sal Glynn,
foster-editor of orphan commas,
red-penciled pal of the politically most sensitive,
and point man with Buck on dangerous sorties into *the wild*.

DISCLAIMER

It is against federal law for any humans (or your neighbors) to possess and/or eat any member of a threatened or endangered species or subspecies in the United States. This law is strictly enforced unless the species is part of the dinner menu for a Friends of Animals fundraiser and pre-approved by the nearest Republican ward chairman, who is also a member of a threatened species.

There are fewer endangered species in the Second and Third World unless you count the two-legged erect species taking the count. Once the proposed merger between the U.S. Peace Corps and the Army Corps of Engineers comes into effect, that will no longer be the case. The loss of any and all open land for the protected critters to crawl on will cause even more of these species to join the swelling ranks of the extinct. Foreign endangered species, live or unlive, can't be imported into the United States; to do so is to be subject to fines of no less than $25. Besides, most regular suitcases are much too small.

TABLE OF CONTENTS

FOREWORD

WHEN NOT interrupted by human nature, Mother Nature provides a healthy, but often violent environment for all her furred and feathered children. For centuries and maybe longer, she has governed the dog-eat-dog natural world. Twentieth century civilization and home entertainment systems have brought about big changes in Mom's household. Rather than patiently waiting out on the back porch after a hard day of chasing cats, today's dog sits comfortably in an air-conditioned condo and listens to his master's voice coming out of an electronic box. Cats have long abandoned the dog-dangerous backyard and are now under secret service protection. Domesticated beasts of burden have been pushed so far outside the urban sprawls that most city kids see horses only as a method of crowd control. Non-domesticated beasts found in the wild are seen as two-dimensional abstractions on the Disney Channel or stalked hungrily by the shrinking numbers of big game hunters higher up on the food chain. With these shenanigans going on, Ms. Nature can barely supervise the barred owl-hump-spotted owl unnatural world.

Unlike an out-of-control American public selfishly gobbling their own weight through a closed circuit food chain in air-conditioned, airbrushed delicatessens, the endangered species described in this cookbook have cordially invited lesser members of their food chain over to have lunch. No, to be lunch. In the same selfless spirit, this cookbook is dedicated to those beleaguered critters of the woods and waters and mountains and molehills. Cursed with Disney-style anthropomorphism so that they may only survive on sweatshirts, they would rather be left alone in their diminishing pristine state and do unto their lessers as we urban humans have done unto them.

INTRODUCTION

THE SUBJECT of endangered species is sizzling hot to touch. The most important thing to know and understand is:

DESTRUCTION AND DEGRADATION OF HABITAT IS THE MOST IMPORTANT CONTRIBUTING FACTOR TO THE ENDANGERMENT OF ANY LIVING THING. THIS IS NOTICEABLE IN THE BEDROOM OF ANY TEENAGER.

With few exceptions, adult teenagers have either overtly or by default approved the destruction of the habitat where endangered species prefer to live and are thoughtfully extending similar sensitive care to the wild new urban wilderness.

The Endangered Species Act of 1973 directs the Secretaries of Commerce and the Interior to determine if a species is in imminent danger of being extinct (endangered) or likely to become endangered in the foreseeable future (threatened). Once a species has been designated, the Act prohibits most anyone from harming or killing it. The U.S. Fish and Wildlife Service is responsible for the implementation of the Endangered Species Act and publishes the listing of the protected plants and animals. Over half of the 1200 plus species currently listed are native to and protected within North America; foreign species benefit from the restrictions placed on importation and sale of the wildlife and derived products in the United States. Individual states may have their own enabling legislation to protect a local delicacy. The selections in this cookbook are conveniently found in the United States and Puerto Rico. With few exceptions, the plants and animals listed within are endangered and the term "species" can mean subspecies or distinct populations.

There are over 3000 new candidates for protection in the United States alone and these will be discussed at the highest government levels, soon after the Federal Department of Dams approves the next power plant site and construction. Filings from the islands have just begun. The large number of listings from the little island of Puerto Rico seems an obvious move to corner the naturalist travel market. Hawaii has so many threatened species that it soon won't be ecologically correct to leave your hotel room, which will suit the room service waiters just fine. Hawaiian tourism officials say that bird watcher interest in its rare exotic songbirds is fast replacing those visitors interested in famous lounge songbirds losing their warble. Regardless of the scores of species nominated for protection status, additions to the listings have slowed in a process encumbered by a polarized public and courageous, responsible politicians who are dedicated to finding the simplest answers to the most complex questions.

GATHERING THE SUPPLIES

CONTEMPORARY culture has evolved from a hunter to a gatherer society. In our predominantly urban culture, it's no longer necessary to hunt for endangered species; they can be gathered right outside your door. In the quasi-military order of settlement, we've pushed the original non-voting furred, scaled, and feathered populations to new frontiers, laid waste (and eggs) in city cores, and then abandoned the scorched earth in an urban sprawl stopped only by the physically immovable. Endangered species now can be found:

AT THE BEACH
Along and in the ocean, lake, pond, and stream.

IN THE BREACH
In transition areas such as wetlands, marshlands, and riparians. Along the road where species habitats and populations have been bisected, trisected, and dissected. Look along both edges of the urban sprawl where urban turns suburban, and where suburban faces off the rural in the meadows, woodlines, and mountaintops.

ANYWHERE THIS EQUIPMENT IS FOUND

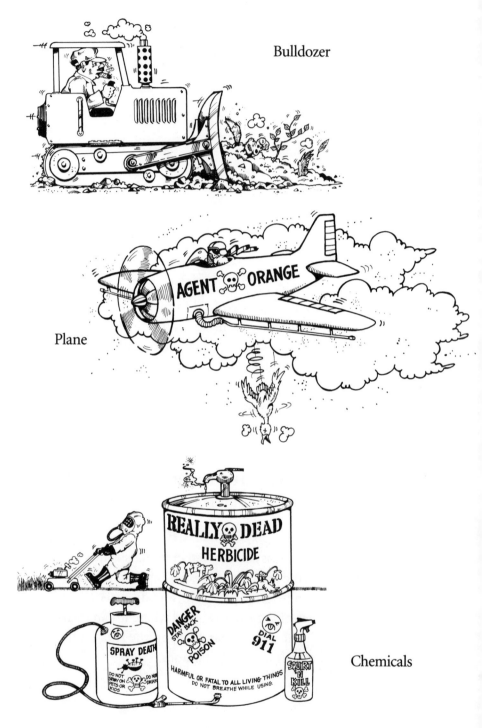

Sign

ANYWHERE WHERE THESE LIVE

Nature Watcher

Domestic Cat

HOW TO PREPARE THE SPECIES

Undress the Little Critter

If your meal has feathers, it's quite likely a bird. Remove feathers. If you eat only eagle breasts, open front to expose breasts (much like a date at the drive-in) and remove. If meat is covered with fur, remove the outer layer as you would a winter snowsuit.

Taking Out the Ugly Stuff

Carefully, repeat, carefully take out all the ishy stuff, including the windpipe, and voice box which contains any last requests. Wash and dry.

HOW TO COOK

You can either eat in or out. Except for French restaurants where entrees are hidden under thick sauces, and most folk eateries in Japan, China, and Taiwan, few restaurants serve endangered species. To eat indoors, you must rely on home cooking. To eat outdoors is to eat the wild in the wild.

At Home

Everything can be baked at 375 degrees or pan-fried until tender or pink. Involve your neighbors. If they are out back sniffing the aromas coming out of your kitchen, discard any incriminating feathered and furred evidence in their dumpsters.

Away From Home

Everything can be roasted over an open fire until pink or tender. It will take a little practice to learn the proper cooking distance from the fire so the outside doesn't burn before the inside bakes.

AMPHIBIANS

E XCEPT FOR the even less popular arachnids who don't understand the full benefits of a federal entitlement program, there are fewer listings for amphibians than any other category. Including the foreigners the feds threw in to cover the lily pad, the current total from all sources is one frog, six toads, and nine salamanders. This short list won't last long; many amphibians, particularly frogs, are croaking all over the word. The three recipes in this section will cover all social occasions.

Golden Coqui

Eleutherodactylus jasperi
Puerto Rico

Too thin-skinned for their own good, frogs have sensitive systems toxins easily penetrate, and the little amphibians are disappearing at an alarming pace almost everywhere. There is no single party at blame for their demise, with the possible exception of bass fishing tournaments.

The golden coqui, an inch-long, brightly-colored resident of Puerto Rico, lives only on the leaf of a mountain plant and is delighted to be the endangered species spokesfrog. This is the only New World frog that bears live young rather than laying eggs; when coqui froggy goes a-courting, only two small clutches of froglets are born. With this slow a birth rate, Puerto Rican sportsfisherman may soon have to switch to angleworms.

GOLDEN FROGS LEGS

Wash frog legs.

Soak in bowl of milk (just enough to cover) for one hour.

Remove from bowl, drain lightly, and sprinkle with salt and pepper.

Roll frog legs in flour and sauté in an open skillet until golden brown.

Texas Blind Salamander

Typhlomolge rathbuni

Texas

This sightless cave-dweller has vestigial eyes marked by two black eye-spots and lives in the underground waters of the limestone caverns of Edwards Plateau, Hays County, Texas.

Salamander eaters prefer the weighty thighs and calves but since this amphibian is only three to four inches long, the entire carcass should be used.

SEEFOOD NEWTBURG

Skin and clean salamanders.

Melt four tablespoons of butter in double boiler.

Add two cups boiled, diced salamander meat.

Cook three minutes.

Add ½ cup dry sherry.

Cook two more minutes.

Add pinch paprika.

Add three beaten chicken egg yolks or 1000 beaten salamander egg yolks.

Cook and stir until thick.

Season with salt and pepper and serve quickly on toast points.

This recipe also works well with the endangered Santa Cruz long-toed, the Shenandoah, and the desert slender salamanders. The Chinese and Japanese giant salamanders are also endangered but then again so is MSG-free Oriental food. With all the endangered stock to choose from, the threatened Cheat Mountain, Red Hills, and San Marcos salamanders will just have to chill a little longer in the salamander colander.

Wyoming Toad

Bufo hemiophyrs baxteri

Wyoming

Found near the Laramie River, this wart-covered amphibian is suffering from herbicide and pesticide overload.

Toad skin contains toxins to make the whole toad less than desirable dinner fare. As toads venture away from their safer marine environment, gulls feed on the breeders and, if asked, the predators agree the best part of a toad is the tongue.

To catch a toad, put a small piece of bright cloth on a hook and dangle in front of the poorly sighted amphibian. Once hooked, carefully remove the extended toad tongue by cutting through the hump from side to side. Repeat procedure until you have more than just a little tongue. Unfortunately, this procedure restricts the surviving toad's diet to inert vegetative matter and requires a new repertoire of less than articulate evening songs.

TONGUE OF TOAD

Preheat oven to 375 degrees.

Scrub tongues well.

Boil one pound of fresh toad tongue for four minutes, skimming scum as needed.

Lower heat and simmer uncovered until tongues are tender.

Drain, skin, and trim roots and gristle as needed.

Arrange tongues in a baking dish and cover them in your favorite toad sauce.

Bake until done.

This recipe can also be used on the endangered Houston toad found licking its brown spots in exclusive Republican enclaves, the Monte Verde, and the threatened Puerto Rican crested toad.

BIRDS

ALTHOUGH WE profess to be a nation of bird lovers, our history makes us look like a bunch of dodos. Our national symbol, the bald eagle, is still squawking about loss of its prime waterfront housing. The slightly less noisy neo-tropical migratory songbirds are in serious, non-specific decline, but any animal that requires both a summer and winter home without holding down two jobs is just asking for trouble. The only birds on an updraft are the Florida snowbird, the brown-headed cowbird, and the grey jailbird. The over 200 birds on the current endangered list are from all habitats. The following selections are representative of most sizes and flavors, plus a few media stars.

American Peregrine Falcon

Falco Peregrinus Anatum
Alaska, Canada, Mexico, South America

The worldwide decline of falcons has been directly linked to the agricultural and industrial uses of pesticides and chemicals passed up the airborne food chain to the not-flying-high-enough falcons, ospreys, and bald eagles. As collected in the fats, the poisons destroy the reproductive process and deliver embryos dead on arrival. Even though there has been a general ban on the use of toxic poisons such as DDT since 1972 in the United States, the use of pesticides in Mexico and South America where peregrines winter affect not only the falcons but also the migratory prey on which they feed.

Peregrines eat more moderate-sized birds like easier-to-swallow swallows, terns, and shorebirds, and are interested in having a taste of the endangered red-cockaded woodpecker before they are all gone. Peregrine falcons will surprise a gull or duck in a two hundred mile-an-hour endorphin-gassed screaming E-dive; in Canada, they have been seen taking a muskrat home for dinner. Surviving muskrats now look up as well as side to side before crossing the pond.

Habitat encroachment has moved falcons from their former important nesting and feeding areas on cliff edges. A few enterprising falcons have made the move to the city and nested in bridges. One famous pair checked in atop a hotel in Salt Lake City where they successfully fledged three young, and qualified for the hotel's family plan. Since egg-eating mountain climbers are prohibited from climbing skyscraping office buildings, falcon nests have been safely placed atop urban high-rises in selected cities. This recovery program has been very successful and threatens to leave the Ford Falcon as the remaining endangered falcon species.

This following recipe is also good for the threatened Arctic peregrine falcon (which may be dropped soon, so hurry) and the endangered Eurasian peregrine.

FALCON FRITTATA

Preheat oven to 375 degrees.

In a mixing bowl, add six eggs (chicken, if nothing else is available), salt and pepper, and two tablespoons of grated Parmesan cheese. Beat well.

Take two cups of diced, cooked falcon breast meat, ¼ cup diced green pepper, and ¼ cup diced sweet onion and add to egg mixture.

Melt two tablespoons of butter in omelet pan.

Add egg mixture to omelet pan and bake in oven until golden brown on top.

Bald Eagle

Haliaeetus leucocephalus

North America, Mexico

Threatened in five states, (Mississippi, Maine, Oregon, Washington, Wisconsin) and endangered in the other forty-three conterminous states, the only eagle unique to North America has been the victim of poisoning. The toxin shock has caused bald eagle groupings to lose even more topknot. Early use of chemicals such as DDT caused the feathered national symbol to lay eggs with shells so thin they'd break once sat on by surrogate U.S. National Park Service biologists. By the time the United States stopped the use of DDT, there were only 800 breeding pairs left in the wild and advocates of making the turkey buzzard the national symbol became reorganized. Protection and specific recovery efforts created a rebound and now there are over six thousand adults alone in over three thousand known nesting sites, three times the number a decade ago.

The primary threat to bald eagles is the loss of nesting habitats to land development. Bald eagles only want quiet isolation along prime shoreline near sprawling urban populations. Bald eagles have been declared illegal to harm since 1940 and protected since 1973; land developers are now required to guarantee non-disturbance zones of seven hundred fifty to fifteen hundred feet from eagle nests and free film at designated photo opportunity sites.

It's also illegal to possess any eagle feathers unless you are a Native American and plan to use them in ceremonial activities, such as decorating the new casino. The possession of eagle down is ipso facto prima facie evidence of an illegal defeathering and the possession of an insulated eagle down jacket is considered further evidence.

BALD EAGLE À LA KING

Preheat oven to 375 degrees.

Pluck and clean one bald eagle.

Smear eagle with olive oil, place in roasting pan along with washed and peeled carrots and potatoes, and roast until done.

The best way to eat the king of birds is like an eagle. Rip and tear the skin for the sweetmeats, craning with majestic malice at the other predators at the table. Once you've had your fill, rip off another chunk and drop into your child's beak. Once your immediate family has had its fill, it's time to fly to allow the smaller birds to ravish the remains.

Brown Pelican

Pelecanus occidentalis

Texas, Louisiana, California

The brown pelican flies along the southern California coastline and plies the airways to enjoy the Atlantic and Gulf coasts. Chemical contaminants in their coastal saltwater habitat have been the principal enemy of the brown pelican. During the late 1950s, pesticide exposure almost eliminated the brown pelican along the Louisiana and Texas coast. In California, one particular downstream island colony failed because a pesticide plant dumped DDT directly in the Los Angeles sewers. The 1972 ban on DDT and prohibitions on the use of the pesticide endrin have been so successful that, except in Louisiana and Texas, the eastern brown populations are no longer protected. Off the western shore, fishermen can still hook a small number of pelicans on shallow-running bait fish or lures. Once on the line, fly fishing takes on a new meaning.

The brown pelican has so much of its head taken up with its bill that there isn't much room left over for a brain. One of the reasons why this bird isn't doing well is that it mistakes heat ripples on highways for water full of fish and dives directly into the tarmac. Those able to walk away from this sudden stoppage can't get back up in the air and have to take the bus to San Diego for additional flight training.

PELICAN PEMMICAN
Find crashed pelican and place it bill down on eight-lane highway.

Allow two days in hot sun and several passes by over-loaded semis to flatten and cure meat into jerky.

Retrieve pelican, remove bones and feathers, and place jerky in a large bowl.

Using a pastry knife, combine jerky with an equal amount of animal fat (beef or pork).

Store in plastic bag in refrigerator until ready to use.

California Condor

Gymnogyps californianus
Oregon, California

With wing spans up to ten feet, the California condor is the largest bird of prey in North America. This bird feeds on leftovers of deer, elk, antelope, and, in a pinch, small animal roadkill. Condors eagerly follow cattle drives, watching for stragglers and occasionally lifting an unsuspecting calf to 100 feet and dropping it, breaking it open like a clam. Unlike other birds, the condor has no natural enemies and they live for as long as forty-five years. Since their neck and head are already bald and grey, it's hard to tell if they age gracefully. Males and females look alike to both the inexperienced eye of junior bird biologists and to the immature condor, which can really upset the nest. Mortality has been associated with sitting on incoming power lines, being contestants in ugliest bird shooting contests, and eating lead-filled birds.

The historic range of the condor was as far as both coasts. By the 1967 listing, its flight path was restricted to California. Almost extinct in the wild, the continent's last condors were finally taken into captivity in 1987. Andean condors were then imported and introduced in 1988 to assist in fine-tuning reentry procedures to the wild for the captive native birds. The current captive population consists of sixty big ugly birds. Seven free spirits are now soaring high and wild over the Los Padres National Forest, safely out of range of the drive-by shootings in south central Los Angeles.

CONDOR BLEU

Preheat oven to 375 degrees.

Pluck and clean condor.

In a large bowl, combine ¼ cup blue cheese, ½ pound chopped proscuitto ham, ½ pound cream cheese and one teaspoon each of oregano, basil, marjoram, and a pinch of tarragon.

Stuff cavity with mixture.

Place stuffed bird in roasting pan in oven and bake until tender.

Serve with hollandaise sauce.

Adult condors feed on slow cooking roadkill and if a female drops an egg in the feeding frenzy, *Highway Huevos* or *Condor Eggs in Concrete* are just what the scavenger ordered. The hot sun cooks the egg; top with a dollop of cream and garnish with chopped green onion. Coddled captive condors provide an endless source of *Coddled Condor Eggs* for captive staff breakfast meetings, another little discussed reason why more condors aren't released into the wild.

Hawaiian Dark-Rumped Petrel

Pterodroma phaeopygia sandwichensis

Hawaii

All birds of Hawaii are more or less in a fix due to a variety of man-made conditions. These captive birds are a very specialized species and often unable to cope with any change. Many island birds didn't even need wings until the tourists showed up. The ground nesters are easy prey to dogs, cats, rats, and pigs and any human movement into a breeding or nesting area by foot or mechanical means is stressful. Birds whose traditional habitat is the shoreline compete unsuccessfully with resort and condo developers whose idea of land stewardship is to sell the first unit to the first steward that walks in.

DARK RUMP ROAST OF PETREL

Preheat oven to 350 degrees.

Pluck and clean petrel.

Using a sharp knife, carefully remove the rump from the carcass. Wash and wipe rump. The remainder of the petrel can be used for soup stocks, gravies, etc.

Dress rump with strips of bacon, place in roasting pan, and bake until butt is brown.

This recipe will also work for Hawaiian Akepa, creeper (Oahu and Molokai creeper, too), Hawaiian common moorhen, coot, duck, hawk, stilt, goose, and crow. Ditto for the Layson duck, Kauai Akialoa and 'O'o, small Kauai thrush, Molokai thrush, Maui Akepa, and the parrotbill. Double ditto for the crested honeycreeper, Nihua Millerbird, finch, and Newell's Townsend Shearwater. Any remaining endangered birds not remembered by this dish will be remembered by the songbirds in the resort hotel lounges warbling something like this:

Aki-apol-alau, Po'ouli, O'o Palila, Nui-cupu'u

Least Tern

Sterna antillarum

North America, Mexico, Caribbean, South America

The smallest, but not really the least in the eyes of their parents, protected least tern nests above the waterline in shallow depressions on sandbars and islands along rivers not rearranged for irrigation or by dams. At best, these nesting depressions provide slight cover from predators. The least this tern can do to survive is alter its breeding habits. Nesting during the hottest summmer days, if Mom tern moves off the nest, the eggs get scrambled and the chicks get quick fried.

During the 1800s, the eastern population of least terns was reduced significantly to put feathers on dress hats. While general protection has increased the overall population, women's hats don't look quite as pretty as before. In the most recent important tern of events, the 1985 federal listing protects only the interior populations and the least tern is not considered endangered when found within fifty miles of the coast.

To do a good tern, add fat to any recipe. Small birds are normally quite dry and beef suet or bacon are popular additives.

A TERN FOR THE WURST

Pluck, clean, and debone tern.

Using a meat grinder, grind tern meat adding ⅓ pound of beef suet for each pound of tern.

Place ground meat into a large mixing bowl and add ½ teaspoon of sage for each pound of meat, and salt and pepper to taste.

Mix thoroughly.

Form mixture into patties and fry until golden brown, or stuff into sausage casings and fry.

This recipe is also good for the endangered California least tern and the roseate tern.

Light-footed Clapper Rail

Rallus longirostris levipes
California

A hen-like marsh bird, the clapper rail doesn't migrate, and is content to stay at home and mind the kids. Destruction of its saltwater habitat by dredging and filling salt marshes is pushing this bird over the edge; so will a good storm or the rat patrol. Danger from the sky is from those northern harriers, the red-tailed hawk and peregrine falcon. These small mud hens even have to watch their step as horse mussels have been reported to trap a rail beak or foot which make the bird even more light-footed.

The rail family includes Virginia, clapper, sora, king, and the common coot. Clappers eat all day long, but these small birds are thin as a rail. For any recipe, you'll need at least six rails.

SMOTHERED MUD HEN

Pluck, clean, and cut up rails. Soak in lightly salted water for one hour.

Fry six bacon strips and save the fat.

Remove rails from water, lightly pat dry, coat with flour, and fry them in a large skillet with the bacon fat until brown. Remove skillet from heat and set aside.

In another skillet, sauté ¼ cup chopped onions, ¼ cup chopped green peppers, and ¼ cup chopped red peppers.

Add one eight-ounce can of cream of mushroom soup and one cup of water to the vegetables.

Salt and pepper vegetable mixture to taste.

Pour vegetable mixture over the rails, cover, and let simmer until rails are tender.

This recipe is good for Yuma clapper, Guam rail, the California clapper, or any of their many island cousins.

Red-Cockaded Woodpecker

Picoides borealis

Southern United States

Listed in 1970, the red-cockaded woodpecker nests in the soft middle of old growth pine trees infected with red-heart disease. Named for the tiny red patch behind the eye of the male that resembles a cockade (a fancy French hat ribbon), this woodpecker lives in clans of up to nine birds with only a single breeding pair. The non-reproducing adults, called helpers, end up as surrogate sons of the dominant male, which really inflames their cockades. A woodpecker colony consists of one to twelve trees, encompassing an area of over one hundred fifty acres in a forest that took over eighty years to grow up into the proper pine habitat. Many states are active in reconstructing the original habitats by allowing proscribed burns to kill the competing hardwood trees; on military reservations, special procedures have been instituted to keep armored tanks from crashing into nesting trees.

Flying squirrels compete for nests so the spokesbird for the red-cockaded woodpeckers recommends we taste the squirrels first (see *Braised Bushytails* recipe). If you're still hungry, try the larger pileated woodpecker who is also vying for the best rent-controlled government nests.

WOODPECKER

The publisher's Decent Recipe Review Board prevented the inclusion of a famous beak recipe for this bird. In any event, remember that the best peckers are those that have tapped poplar or willow trees when the sap is not running.

Spotted Owl

Strix occidentalis caurina
California, Oregon, Washington

Wise old media owls will recognize that the spotted owl is not even an endangered subspecies, but old growth activists threatened to spike the author if the threatened bird was omitted from this cookbook. The northern spotted owl has been blinded by so many media kleig lights of late that their night vision is endangered and have alerted their Mexican species-mates to the perils of popularity.

Spotted owls do not build nests, using instead pre-existing cavities, such as nearly empty logger billfolds in old growth forests, to raise their young. They eat rabbits and woodrats and have requested nesting information on the troubled San Francisco flying squirrel. The great horned owl is a threat to the livelihood of the adult spotted owl and the life of the spotted owlettes. The barred owl is invading the historic spotted owl range, competing for food and cover and, worse yet, seeking romantic involvement.

With its sharp beak and talons, be sure the owl is truly dead before cooking. A sure indication is when it doesn't give a hoot anymore. You can skin and bake the entire bird for hors d'oeuvres. If you leave the skin on, shadows of the original spots will highlight this distinguished bird from the lesser birds sitting around your table.

The following recipes have been designated an indicator series by the U.S. Fish and Wildlife Service test kitchens. A properly prepared spotted owl is an indication of how good the other large threatened birds taste.

SPOTTED SKIDDER SNACKS

Pluck and clean spotted owl.

Calk owl. Stepping on an owl in calk boots will soften any mature owl. For an acceptable pâté, an extended jig is recommended.

Smear owl pieces with olive oil and roast in either a 350 degree oven or over an open fire until done.

VARIATION

Deep fry owl parts in either vegetable or bar oil until golden brown.

Slice with a crosscut or small chain saw and serve.

CHOKER CHICKS

Sure to please the young loggers at any table. Check the rigging of the choker for any nesting young owls. Roast over an open slash fire.

For the more independent timber wolf, an adult spotted owl can be slow-roasted for sandwich meat.

GYPO GYROS

Arrange on vertical spit pieces of owl and alternate with slices of well-marbled murrelet.

Roast in either a 350 degree oven or over an open fire until done.

Remove pieces from spit, slice thin, and place in open pita bread along with slices of tomato, avocado, and pickle, and a leaf or two of lettuce torn into small pieces.

The colorful feathers can be used in tying flies to catch the Pacific Northwest steelhead, a favorite dish of the spotted owl, which puts a nice spin on the food chain.

The Mexican spotted owl has been proposed for listing and, if approved, a management plan to preserve old growth burritos will be required.

Whooping Crane

Grus Americana
North America, Mexico

In the 1800s and early 1900s, these large, tall birds with wing-spans that can stretch over seven feet, lost important nest-ing and winter habitat, lots of feathers to the military trade, and an occasional tailfeather to a hapless goose hunter. By the early 1940s, there were fewer than twenty birds left. Subsequent protection was so successful that a major childhood cough was named after the crane by the U.S. pharmaceutical industry, the sound of the cough resembling the cry the whooping crane made when being plucked for hat feathers. Cranes now nest in protected Canadian refuges and winter in similar refuges in Texas. During the mid-1970s, scientists at the protected breeding centers shipped eggs to Idaho to put in surrogate nests of sandhill cranes. Successfully raised by the non-endangered sandhill cranes, these confused young whooping cranes now winter with the sandhills in New Mexico.

Whooping cranes mate for life and are well-known for their courtship dance. To make whoopie (and little whoopies), cranes first whoop it up with dances full of flapping, head-bowing, leaps, and loud noises, making the whooping crane an obvious candidate as a symbol for any adult service club.

Since the average whooping crane weighs at least three times as much as a wild goose, plan on spending three times as much energy plucking the bird. Prepare three times as much wild rice stuffing. Cook it three times as long as an Aleutian Canada goose.

The Aleutian Canada goose is another natural kidder who has filed for and been granted federal protection in both its breeding and nesting grounds. A small subspecies of the common Canada goose, the *branta canadensis leucopareia* are typically marked with a white ring at the base of the neck. Their major decline came from the introduction of Arctic fox into the Alaskan breeding areas by the Russians and Americans in the early 1800s and the main breeding area, Buldir Island in the western Aleutians, is one of the few island without furry egg-eaters and home of one of the three remaining nesting populations.

It's difficult to distinguish the Aleutian Canada goose from another subspecies, the non-threatened cackling Canada goose. When flying over confused goose hunters wary of game wardens, these natural kidders have been suspected of cackling until out of range of the long guns. Prepared in proportion to the following crane recipe, he who cooks his Aleutian Canada goose first cackles last.

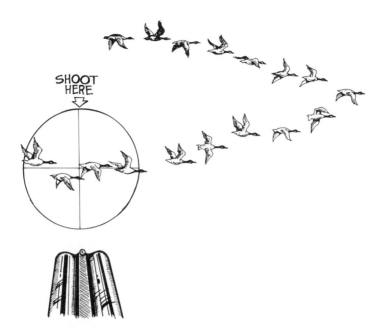

Other notes

The youngest and most tender geese are in the back of the formation.

ROAST WHOOPING CRANE

Preheat oven to 375 degrees.

Pluck and clean crane.

Stuff cavity with wild rice mixture. If using raisins or currants in the stuffing, remember to soak them in warm water one hour before making up the stuffing.

Place stuffed bird in roasting pan in oven and bake until tender.

FISHES

THE FISH LIST is mostly made up of threatened little non-game fish that only want their waterhole back. With all the changes in habitat, those fish removed for captive breeding find it difficult to go home again. Private and public money is not as available for anything less than a wild, native stock steelhead or salmon; hard-pressed fisheries officials are lobbying to have the mammal restoration dollars assigned to their little non-game checking accounts.

The recent listing of the Snake River sockeye salmon should be no surprise to those who have witnessed the rapid decline of the species and population of native fisheries. Any fish who swims the streams has been particularly hard hit, but only because we haven't figured out how to dam the offshore.

Alabama Cavefish

Speoplatyrhinus poulsoni
Alabama

A three-inch-long eyeless cave dweller with transparent skin and fins, the Alabama cavefish is one of the rarest freshwater fishes in North America and, with fewer than one hundred survivors, certainly the rarest American cavefish. This big-hearted albino lives only in Key

Cave, part of an Alabama limestone formation. As in many other caves, the poop (or guano) of the endangered grey bat is the bottom of the food chain and the survival (and regularity) of the grey bat is critical to the survival of the cavefish. (This connection is so important that the Alabama State Department of Dingbats has tried to cultivate guano in the lab; so far it's only available in the employee cafeteria.) Natural flooding washes this and other organic matter into and around the bat cave, providing food for the fauna, which in turn feed the small invertebrates the cavefish enjoy.

The Alabama cavefish's head takes up over a third of its three-inch length, leaving a meager two inches of prime guano-flavored cavefish fillets (make that an inch once the tail has been lopped off). Once you run a knife down the backbone to remove the slabs of meat, you'll have just enough to feed the seldom sighted Alabama cavecat, who doesn't need a recipe.

Amber Darter

Percina antesella
Georgia, Tennessee

The diminutive amber darter lives in the quiet, gentle riffles over sand and gravel in the Conasauga River Basin in Georgia and Tennessee. While some of the river runs through safer national forest waters, other parts of watershed are subject to potentially harmful alterations such as those caused by under-inflated float tube parties of bottom-dragging, really big people. Even swimmers and divers disturb enough algae to upset the small defenseless darter. A common darter physical ailment is gas bubble disease, a nitrogen buildup in the tissues similar to the bends, caused by the spring run-offs of sewage. Even a good darter farter can't pass this gas.

In the late 1970s, the infamous snail darter was the focus of much controversy as it halted the completion of the Tennessee Valley Authority's Tellico Dam on the Little Tennessee River. The small darter was listed as endangered in 1975, with the river designated as the critical survival habitat. The proposed dam would have flood the homes of the snail darters and, in 1977, a federal appeals court ruled that it could not be completed, a decision upheld by the U.S. Supreme

Court the following year. In response, Congress amended the Endangered Species Act in 1978, and created a review committee that could give exemptions to the act for resource development which was in irreconcilable conflict with any pork barrel project in a key voter state. The committee could determine whether a species lived or died, yet they too upheld stopping construction of the dam. In 1979, an amendment exempting the dam from the act was quietly attached as a rider in yet another sleeping Congressional session, creating the first federal decision to endanger a species.

The Fish and Wildlife Service tried transplanting the darter in nearby waters prior to the dam being completed. That relocation has done well and other small thriving populations have since been discovered.

In recently released court documents regarding the litigation of the Tellico Dam, a snail darter recipe was found among the blueprints of the dam.

DARTER SAUCE

Wash and clean one school of darters.

Run cleaned darters through water turbines to pound the fish into smooth paste. Let stand to cool.

In medium-size mixing bowl, combine one tablespoon of darter paste to one tablespoon each of chopped sweet pickles and chopped onion, and one teaspoon of minced parsley. Mix well.

Add one cup of mayonnaise and blend. Chill and serve.

Good as a dip for all species. You can also use the endangered boulder, fountain, Maryland, watercress, or Okalousa darter and the threatened leopard, Niangua, and bayou darter. This is the best darter sauce by a dam site.

Colorado Squawfish

Ptychocheilus lucius
United States, Mexico

The Colorado squawfish is the largest minnow found in North America. Once commercially sold as white salmon, the squawfish used to reach up to six feet long, but now seldom grows longer than three feet. Dam construction on the Colorado River and other water diversions have blocked migrations and there is evidence of further decline due to the introduction of non-native predatory fish and fish imposters. Squawfish are easily fooled with flashily dressed flies and lures in the Green River in Utah, and the Yampa and Colorado Rivers in Colorado and Utah.

The squawfish is the adopted symbol of the John Denver Big Rock Candy Mountain High Screech Music Museum, which is assembling life lore for a feature film to be produced by the Sundunce Studio entitled, "Squawfish That No Longer Runs Through It."

To survive in the increasingly unisex fishing environment, the Colorado squawfish has physically evolved and the following recipe has been tailored to meet this rapid natural change.

SQUAWFISH BALLS

In a large pot, boil one pound of squawfish fillets. Let cool, then pound and chop the fillets.

Sauté one medium minced onion in one tablespoon of butter.

In a large mixing bowl, combine the onion, two beaten eggs, one teaspoon of lemon juice, a dash of prepared mustard, and the chopped fillets. Mix well.

Form the mixture into balls, roll into cracker crumbs, and deep fry in vegetable oil until golden brown.

VARIATION   Alaska native tribal elders prepare a television snack called squaw candy to accompany the attention given to the National Geographic Society specials on Eskimo life. Fresh salmon bellies are soaked in a salt brine and the strips laid out on smoking racks to dry. A similar white meat recipe is perfect for the squaws fished from the Colorado and Green Rivers.

Devils Hole Pupfish

Cyprinodon diabolis
Nevada

The thermal springs found seventy-five miles northwest of Las Vegas at Ash Meadows in Nye County, Nevada has the highest concentration of endemic plants and animals in the United States. Both the Devils Hole and Warm Springs pupfish and the Ash Meadows speckled dace are found in these springs. The habitat of the spring ponds is threatened by the pumping of ground water for development, risking the growth of the pupfish into an adult dogfish. Then again, everything in Nevada is a gamble.

If you don't want to use this perfect bait for gamefishing, block one of the thermal spring ponds for an eco-bath; using a hairnet, you can trap a small quantity of these little puppies trying to escape your soapy waters. For a doggone good meal, try the following recipe.

HUSHED PUPPIES (PUPPIEFISH)

In a large mixing bowl, combine one cup of cornmeal, one teaspoon of double-acting baking powder, ½ teaspoon of salt, three tablespoons of minced onion (or four tablespoons if you like more bite than bark), one beaten egg, and ½ cup of milk. Mix well.

Clean and rinse pupfish. Deep fry fish in vegetable oil, remove and let drain.

Form dough around snuffed pups, then deep fry again until golden brown.

Remove from oil, let drain, and serve.

This recipe can be used for the endangered Ash Meadow Amargosa, Commanche Springs, desert, Leon Springs, and Owens pupfish. For a combined species Ash Mountain fry fry, capture and clean the speckled dace and prepare as above. That experience can be used for the endangered Kendall Warm Spring, Moapa, the threatened black side, desert, Foskett speckled, spike, and little Colorado spine daces.

Humpback Chub

Gila cypha

Arizona, Colorado, Utah, Wyoming

Humpback chubs can get as long as sixteen inches and weigh up to two pounds. This uniquely shaped minnow-like fish was designed to roam in the same historic rough waters as the squawfish and now are found only in the more turbulent deep canyons of the Colorado River system. When the Flaming Gorge Dam in Utah and the Glen Canyon dam in Arizona were built, chubs disappeared both up and down river.

Similar to the cheeks of the saltwater halibut, the humps of this endangered non-game fish are the most prized. Sad tales of hump poachers are rising to the surface and illegal trading in chubby humps is rumored to be directed by the Gambusia family of Nevada. Local taverns near the Colorado River will serve the delicacy when available; away from mom's apron strings and reckless with stolen coffee money, non-resident fishermen try to buy more than one hump at a seating. Due to federal protections, it's difficult to get more than one hump from a server per day and impossible to buy, much less print the recipe.

This advice is obviously not useful for the endangered hump-deprived Bonytail chub, Borax Lake chub, Mohave tui and Owen's tui chub, Pahranagat roundtail chub, and the Yaqui and Virgin River chub. Ditto to the threatened Chihuahua, Hutton tui, slender, Sonora, and spotfin chub.

Short-Nose Suckers

Chasmistes brevirostris

California, Oregon

Belying the P.T. Barnum adage, "There is a sucker born every minute," these short-nosed suckers have been thrown out of their historic homes on the bottoms of the Klamath River Basin. Dams, dredging, and diverting have blocked the spawning runs and no young fish are being born, resulting in a remaining population of old suckers.

In most households, suckers are best fixed by burying in the compost pile and then going to the local fish and chips place for a good meal. Ditto for the endangered Lost River, June, razorback, dwarf Modoc, and threatened Warner suckers. The June sucker has been bullied about by the white bass and walleye, while the dwarf sucker is interbreeding with the Sacramento sucker. It's particularly embarrassing to the California Fish and Game Department that four out of five endangered suckers are from their state. The Cui-ui, an endangered sucker found only in Nevada, is not unusual; with the end of the go-go 1980s, more endangered suckers will come from that state.

Trout

The few trout that swim through the threatened list are there as much for weak moral resolve as habitat destruction. The lack of discretion shown in most trout streams is contaminating the species' gene pool. For example, the endangered Apache fools around with brown trout, the threatened Little Kern golden and the Paiute cutthroat with the rainbow. The human damage done to spawning areas for both the Lahontan and greenback cutthroat is insignificant compared to the antics of the brown-spotted stranger in the brook bedroom.

It's difficult to choose a recipe that works for any of these crossbreeds, much less a species-specific fishing tackle. And if that is not enough, the restoration of the Gila trout in New Mexico and Arizona has been so successful that you soon won't know if you're eating an endangered or threatened species. What's a catch and clean fisherperson to do?

In an effort to use the entire fish, fly fishing purists donate trout fishheads for habitat fundraisers. The following recipe was created specially for this thoughtful contribution.

TROUT HEAD SOUP

Clean and wash six fish heads. Remove gills, eyes, lips, and teeth.

Pan fry heads in two tablespoons of olive oil in a large open skillet.

Add to skillet two chopped medium-size onions, three diced potatoes, and two sliced tomatoes. Add more olive oil if necessary.

Prepare three cups of white sauce and add to skillet. Season with salt and pepper and simmer for thirty minutes.

Serve in individual bowls.

When their fellow anglers are downstream, trout fisherman squeeze the eggs out of the big females for a river repast.

ROE N' YOUR BOAT
(Gently Down the Stream)

Rinse eggs in cool water, then boil for fifteen minutes, let cool and drain.

Roll eggs in flour.

Using an open skillet, fry eggs in olive oil until done.

Serve piping hot.

Northern California Special Report: The Nature Conservancy has dedicated a section of the McCloud River for recovery of a star of the Grand Old Fishery, the Dolly Varden. This chary member of the trout family is noted for its hourglass figure and each corporate sponsor is assured exclusive fishing box seats should a sighting occur.

MAMMALS

BY DEFINITION, a mammal nourishes its young by milk. By definition, an endangered mammal is one that gets up in the morning. Once the English-speaking mammals stood up and headed west by wagon train, interest in the welfare of our four-legged friends diminished. Once they circled the wagons and learned how to pour concrete, any concern for the furred mammals vanished. Even the large rodents are being threatened; the Vancouver Island marmot is only an alpine speedbump to ski resort developers mind-schussing high mountain marmot habitat. And who will save the Australian hairy-nosed wombat?

Too often, only the most photogenic mammals of "charismatic megafauna" have their own funds and societies. Size can be a determining qualifier; the awe-inspiring great whales will always have bumper stickers. Any hairy animal that looks remotely like your meat man and lives in a mist will always generate movie scripts for undernourished actresses. But who will speak for the threatened Utah prairie dog once the re-introduced endangered black-footed ferret gobbles its way through all the Wyoming cousins? And who will slow the foreign entries before the Argentinians add another pink fairy armadillo?

It's always been the white person's missionary zeal that organizes someone else's backyard. It's easier to find support for the endangered Nigerian red-eared, nose-spotted monkey than to import a good moderately priced long-leaf cigar. The larger mammals in this section wish to extend their home grown appreciation for your early support.

Alabama Island Beach Mouse

Peromyscus polionotus ammobates
Alabama

Beach mice are small-bodied, hairy-tailed, bulgy-eyed, big-eared, sand-colored beach bums. The Alabama Island beach mouse plays peaceably under the moonlight on a barrier island off northeast Florida. Juveniles develop quickly on the beach, reaching sexual maturity in as little as six weeks or before the end of school vacation. The beach front real estate boom and dune buggies fueled with all sorts of alcohol have forced these original citizens out of their beach burrows, making room for the new domestic house mice and a jogging track for pet cats.

MOUSE DIP

Clean and skin several beach mice. Mouse intestines
and other interior organs can be removed through the

opening under the tail. Rinse well to remove all sand particles.

Place cleaned mice in boiling salted water until done. Remove mice and chill.

Carefully pack mouse bodies with pre-cooked seasoned dressing (both wild rice and bread crumb stuffings work well). Arrange stuffed mice in a deep serving dish, allowing the tails to drape over the edge.

Cover the arranged stuffed mice with your favorite mouse mousse and chill again, then serve.

Other endangered beach bums are the tasty Choctawhatchee and the Perdido Key beach mouse, the Key Largo cotton mouse, and the Salt Marsh harvest mouse. The threatened Anastasia Island beach mouse will have to wait.

If there aren't enough mice to feed all your guests, add a few endangered voles, which are mouse-like rodents with shorter tails. To capture the southwestern flavor of its endangered habitat, the Amargosa and the Hualapai vole are best prepared using *Vole Mole*, the popular Mexican recipe of native peppers with a chocolate twist.

If you still feel rodent-deprived, add the endangered giant, Stephens', Tipton, Morro Bay, and Fresno kangaroo rat, all of them California residents. While only six ounces, a kangaroo rat can get up to fourteen inches in length; you'll need a very deep serving dish unless you prepare only the meaty hind legs used for hopping through its native grasslands. Hop on this food source as poisons used to control the ground squirrel and owls with eating disorders are taking its toll on this rat.

Black-Footed Ferret

Mustela nigripes
Western United States, Western Canada

This little weasel (whose main food is the prairie dog) had almost disappeared from the wild when, in 1987, the Wyoming Fish and Game Department captured the last eighteen known ferrets for breeding. Under the watchful eye of the Wyoming Catholic diocese, the now-protected ferrets practiced rhythm birth control and over 300 of the little rascals came from out of nowhere. Sensitive to the feelings of the prairie dogs, the ferret dieticians tried to teach the captive ferrets to feed on non-furred food groups such as broccoli and espresso grounds, but to no avail. More importantly, the researchers had to ensure that the ferrets didn't learn to like and imitate people; junior staffers were forced to crawl down artificial burrow holes and compete for meat to reinforce the ferrets' natural proclivities. When prairie dogs couldn't be captured for pen food, the captive weasels had to eat abandoned domestic dogs trapped near the town square in Jackson Hole. In 1991, forty-nine ferrets were reintroduced late at night in large areas full of white-tailed prairie dogs (ferrets need over one hundred acres of prairie dog colony each to survive). The new weasels on the block are having difficulties trying to remember how to eat a prairie dog, while keeping an eye to the ground for equally hungry coyotes and badgers, and an eye to the sky for absolutely famished bald eagles and great horned owls. In the fall of 1992, another ninety animals were released and biologists are confirming at least a twenty percent survival rate a month after release. Unconfirmed reports say that coyotes are having a hard time passing the radio telemetry collars found on the captive-bred ferrets.

FERRETS AND CARROTS

Preheat oven to 375 degrees.

Skin and clean ferret.

In a large bowl, combine one cup of your favorite stuffing with ¼ cup chopped carrots.

Stuff cavity with mixture.

Place stuffed ferret in roasting pan in oven and bake until golden brown.

FERRETS FOIS PRAIRIE GRAS

Bake ferret as above without stuffing.

Take baked ferret from oven, allow to cool, and remove meat from bones.

Using a meat grinder, grind the meat.

In a large mixing bowl, combine ground meat with ½ teaspoon each of oregano, basil, and marjoram. Salt and pepper to taste. If the meat is dry, add a little beef suet to help it bind.

Carolina Northern Flying Squirrel

Glaucomys sabrinus coloratus

North Carolina, Tennessee

Flying squirrels actually glide, not fly, using a membrane attached to their limbs along the body. Most flying squirrels species are found in Eurasia; only two occur in North America—the northern flying squirrel (north and west) and the smaller southern flying squirrel (eastern United States).

Unlike most foodstuffs found in-flight, flying squirrels are tasty, nutritious, and can be attractively presented. If pre-packaged foods make you squirrelly, let a tree rodent glide to your plate.

Undress the squirrel by making an incision up under and in the middle of its fur coat without puncturing the belly. Once there is enough room for both hands on opposing sides of the incision, pull the skin off, and sever the head, hands, and feet when resistance is encountered. Eviscerate animal, cleaning body cavity well with fresh water. Parboil for several hours.

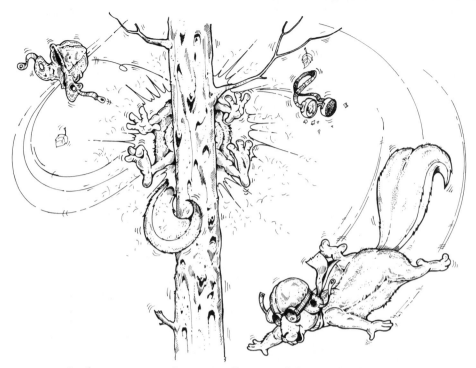

In due respect to the squirrel's natural diet and habitat, stuff the animal with dressing made of pre-cooked acorns, the squirrel's favorite meal, or try the following recipe.

BRAISED BUSHYTAILS

Preheat oven to 350 degrees.

Skin and clean squirrel, then separate into legs, breast, etc.

In a large skillet, brown body parts in three tablespoons of melted butter.

Remove browned body parts and place in roasting pan. Add ½ cup full-bodied red wine and cover. Bake until tender.

Make simple gravy from drippings, pour over meat and serve.

This recipe is also good for the endangered, larger, and maybe tastier Delmarva Peninsula fox squirrel which needs large park-like forests to survive. A single home range can exceed fifty acres, which reduces their survival chances by multiples of fifty. Also good for the endangered Mount Graham red and the Virginia northern flying squirrel.

Florida Panther

Felis concolor coryi

Louisiana, Arkansas, South Carolina, Florida

With fewer than fifty panthers left in the Everglades and the Big Cypress Swamp of Florida, this recipe page may be removed by the publisher before presstime. Reacting to years of bedtime stories of big cats eating small children, dysfunctional developers are paving the habitat necessary for this animal to survive. Important gene studies have discovered another potential threat to the panther's endangered status; the surviving panthers may be the offspring of South American crossbreds released in the 1960s and the federales require a "pure" panther. A federal Swat team composed of immigrant Serbs are standing by for necessary ethnic cleansing.

Originally hunted by native Americans, the panther is now the Florida state animal. To avoid losing at least one big cat a year to roadkill, the state highway department has recommended that any new road construction include protected panther crossings, added animal underpasses, and high fences on the parkways in south Florida. Panthers prefer that the feline fast tracks go directly through the back door of roadside deer parks and have snarled for an open season on the endangered Florida key deer.

Panthers stalk deer, armadillos, and wild hogs. After a big kill, panthers eat up to ten pounds, cover the rest with dirt and debris and return for snacks until the meal is no longer fit to eat. Adding a little heat, you could cook worse.

PIT PANTHER

Dig a pit deep and wide enough to fit the cat, which can reach six feet in length. Line pit with flat rocks, then a layer of loose rocks. Cover with driftwood or any dead hardwood and ignite. Burn off and remove embers and top layer of hot rocks. Quickly cover with quart of water and layer of vegetation. Place cleaned animal plus favorite vegetables in pit, cover with more greens, another layer of vegetables, another layer of greens, then a tarp or canvas. Cover with dirt and debris and do not return until the meal is fit to eat. Cooking takes about 20 minutes per pound and dressed weight ranges from 40 to 100 panther pounds. Leave the tail hanging out, and you'll have a handy reference spot for the meat thermometer to register the preferred temperature of 190 degrees.

This advice can also be used with the endangered jaguar or jaguarundi but many jaguar fanciers aren't interested now that Ford

Motor Company owns them. The smaller ocelot, endangered in Arizona and Texas, and the spotted Margay of Mexico have fine feline fillets under fine feline wraps. The endangered eastern cougar, not seen since 1920, is most likely extinct and if available, is found in New Brunswick stew.

Grey Wolf

Canis lupus

United States (except Minnesota), Mexico

The largest of the dog family, the male grey wolf weighs an average ninety pounds with the female weighing slightly (and more fashionably) less. One of the only two canis species native to North America, the grey wolf was the animal that not only illegally stalked, but also harassed, Little Red Riding Hood. Long thought to be a male, the Big Bad Wolf was discovered in a recent exhumation to be a manly-looking she-wolf recruiting young women to run with her. This revelation has caused a lot of consternation, which just goes to show you—Mom Nature is such a kidder.

At your leisure, skin and dress out the wolf as you would a German shepherd or a dim-witted Irish setter. There is no leisure in this wolf-eat-domesticated-animal world; wolves wolf down their meals,

ripping through the skin to snack on the warm, soft fast foods found in the belly, and then on to the stringier muscle groups. There is no conclusive evidence that a wolf prefers the fillets over the flank steaks of a rancher's calf. There have been isolated reports that the wolf does enjoy the smaller canus owned by dogmatic visitors wearing "Save the Wolves" sweatshirts. Most carnivores, especially those living near Yellowstone, agree that to put on the dog, a culinary constellation of canine cutlets is the universal favorite.

CANIS MAJOR

Skin, clean, and butcher wolf.

In a Chinese wok, heat three tablespoons of peanut oil.

To the heated oil, add one cup of thinly sliced wolf meat, ½ cup of bean sprouts, ½ cup of sliced green pepper, and ½ cup of sliced wild mushrooms.

Stirfry until all ingredients are cooked through.

Serve hot on a bed of crushed dog biscuits.

This recipe is also good for the red wolf. This beleaguered dog was finally removed from the wild to protect them from, among other distractions, interbreeding with the fast-talking coyotes. Red wolves don't pack like the grey wolves and should they lose their mate for life, they will consider all other offers, with the notable exception of advances from the great horny owl. Over a hundred purebreds and red wolves live in government protected breeding facilities and a few select island establishment sites in the southeast. When beckoned by coyotes, the wolves have yipped through their spokesdog that "We'll come out when we are good and ready."

The Chinese are canis connoisseurs and have turned Rin Tin Tin into won ton ton for centuries. During the dog days of summer, Chinese corned dogs (the source of inspiration for the American county fair staple) are thought to relieve heat prostration. Other Asian traditions include scents and flavorings extracted from domestic pets, with anus of canis used liberally before meeting the in-laws.

Your favorite dog recipes can also be used for the endangered San Joaquin kit fox. The smallest and rarest of the canines, this kit fox subspecies numbers under 10,000 and lives in a state which has managed to squeeze everyone into single-digit percentages of their original habitat. The little dog inhabits the Carrizo Plain, half-way between Los Angeles and San Francisco, and are threatened by droughts and the immigration of the red fox, three times as large and given to enjoying midday kit katches. In between dodging coyotes, kit foxes eat rabbits, ground squirrels, kangaroo rats, lizards, and would enjoy hearing from any endangered field mice nearby. The availability of the northern swift fox is unsure; it lives in the United States where it's not protected and protected in Canada where it's not living, a borderline case if there ever was one.

Key Deer

Odocoileur virginianus clavium
Florida

The diminutive key deer eats the decorative shrubs around housing developments on the lower keys of southern Florida and has no natural enemies, unless you count delivery trucks, tourists with fully insured rental cars, free-ranging domestic dogs, poachers, and deep drainage ditches.

The two most important threats to the key deer are the chronic loss of the pine rock land and tropical hardwood hammock habitat of Big Pine Key and the excessive use of the roads crossing this historic stomping grounds. Approximately fifty animals are bumped off the roads each year, almost as many as are born.

The average key deer stands just two feet at the shoulder; the average male weighs eighty pounds and the female just a little less at sixty-five pounds. An inspired road stew made from key parts baked in a crusty pie, fashionably striped with fresh yellow lime slices will take the brakes off your appetite.

KEY YELLOW LIME PIE
Preheat oven to 350 degrees.
Prepare a two-part pie crust.
Skin, clean, and butcher deer.
In a large mixing bowl, combine two cups of cooked (braised, boiled, or baked) deer meat, one cup of thinly

sliced potatoes, one medium-size chopped onion, ½ cup sliced carrots, and one cup of gravy made from deer drippings.

Mix well and season with salt and pepper to taste.

Fill pie crust with mixture. Place top crust on mixture, crimp edges to seal, and poke holes with fork.

Bake until crust is browned (about one hour) and serve.

This recipe is also good for the endangered Sonorian antelope, the soon-to-be-only-threatened Colombian white-tailed deer, and, if you have a really big pie tin, for the threatened woodland caribou.

Virginia Big-Eared Bat

Plecotus townsendii virginianus
Kentucky, North Carolina, West Virginia, Virginia

Since bats are unusually sensitive to any changes in the homey atmosphere of their nesting caves, tourists, spelunkers, and frat parties have caused endangered bats to abandon their traditional roosts and seek shelter elsewhere. The local humane societies have closed their temporary shelters saying, "Bats, we don' need no stinkin' bats!" If disturbed in the bat cave during hibernation, the bat's precious stored fats are burned and cannot be replaced in an insect-free winter, causing the bat to starve. Bats can eat half their weight daily in mosquitoes, making a good argument for the state of Minnesota to import bats to eat their state bird. Bats are also responsible for long-haired farm women abandoning the open fields for the kitchen to practice the endangered skill of baking a pie with a truly flaky crust.

While less than one percent of bats can carry rabies, avoid eating sick bats. It's difficult to take a temperature of an active bat—use a rectal thermometer when they are just hanging around the house. Coughing, sneezing, crashing into walls, or flying in full daylight are telltale signs of a sick winged rodent.

The most recognizable part of a bat is its screech, heard just before its slightly dull fangs jam into the neck of its latest victim, but you can't eat the screech.

Clean bats as you would a small diving duck like a merganser, gutting and removing undesirable parts. The wings are already as tough as old shoe leather, and properly tanned can be used to make coin purses or baby shoes. The head is best cut off, jarred in an alcohol solution and sent in an unmarked box to your mother-in-law (another old bat) for her birthday. The remaining carcass is enough to feed one small adult if accompanied with portions of other federally protected furred food groups.

With dressed weights barely clearing half an ounce, the most popular bat recipe will required an experienced bat boy to shag a cave full of bat breasts.

BATS IN THE BELFRY

Skin, clean, and cut bat breasts into narrow strips.

In a large open skillet, fry strips until medium rare. Save any drippings and wipe skillet dry.

Julienne one each yellow, green, and red bell pepper.

Add two tablespoons olive oil to skillet and fry peppers until lightly cooked. Lower heat and add strips and drippings.

Cover skillet and cook until done.

Serve hot and garnish with guano.

This recipe can be used for the endangered gray bat, the Indiana bat, the Mexican long-nosed bat, the Ozark big-eared bat, and the Sanborn long-nosed bat. In the wild, bats act as pollinators. The Sanborn's long-nosed bat feeds on cactus nectar, migrating and pollinating along the way until they get to the agave plant, the source of tequila and the source of telltale abnormal human behavior in Southern California. The Hawaiian hoary bat is a rare, native subspecies of a mainland bat. The major problem with the ope'a pe'a is that it's so secret (active only at twilight when most Hawaiians are still poi-groggy) that it's difficult to tell if the bat has a health problem, much less be a part of the traditional Hawaiian bat luau.

Florida West Indian Manatee

Trichechus manatus

Southeastern United States, Caribbean Sea, South America

The manatee, or sea cow, is found in the rivers and streams of the Gulf States but mostly favor Florida's brackish waters. The manatee has been designated the Florida state marine mammal and the state is now a manatee refuge and sanctuary. To harm the beast is a second degree misdemeanor, punishable by a state fine of $500 and/or the confiscation of the boaters half-rack of beer and bag of Beernuts.

First reported in North America by Christopher Columbus, the manatee was hunted by Native Americans and Spaniards for the thick skin used in making canoes, war shields and, less successfully, condoms. Manatees are quite social in the water and, in between mammoth vegetarian snacks, hug and kiss each other. Thought to be the basis for the original reports of mermaids, any romanticized vision of mammals that can reach 2,000 pounds must have been seen through a mist of acquavit by a Swedish fishing fleet. Fortunately for the sea cow gene pool, the female manatees wisely showed no interest in the Swedish seamen.

Manatees are threatened by habitat deterioration and boating accidents. The mammals are so sensitive that a drop in water temperature to sixty degrees can throw these vegetarians off their feed. About one-third of the couple of hundred mortalities a year are caused by boat and barge collisions. Speed limits have been put on sportboaters and mosquito boats must rely on sonar detectors for any underwater cow cops in the area.

Flood control gates can squeeze seacows too tight and provide a sea cowboy an opportunity to rustle up some grub.

ROASTED MANATEE HAMS

Preheat oven to 325 degrees.

Skin, clean, and butcher manatee. Slice off a five-pound ham.

The slices in the ham made by speedboats can be used, instead of marking the ham, for a natural decorative touch.

Place cloves in the slices.

Place ham in roasting pan and bake until the ham has an internal temperature of 160 degrees.

Serve by carving the ham into half-inch-thick steaks, covering them with a dead-eye gravy made from the drippings.

This recipe can also be used on the endangered Amazonian manatee and the threatened West African manatee, which speedboaters on the Senegal River say doesn't taste as good as a mammal that is endangered. A Hawaiian version of this recipe using pineapple slices as garnish can be also used in preparing the endangered Hawaiian monk seal.

Whales

Whales have had an active press relations program for a number of years, but it wasn't until 1986 that members of the International Whaling Commission voted for a complete moratorium on whaling, with the intention of phasing it out completely. The agreements are under tension. Whale bones were once used in corset stays and since the ban on whaling, unemployed whalers have argued that women's figures have suffered accordingly. The following eight whales are now protected from any boat making more than f-stops.

Gray Whale

Eschrichtius robustus

This mid-sized baleen whale is a slow swimmer and usually covered by encrustations on its back. The gray whale migrates over 10,000 miles round trip, from feeding grounds in Alaskan waters to breeding grounds off Baja and Mexico. There were once three breeding groups but the Atlantic gray was hunted to extinction in the 17th century. The two remaining groups consist of several hundred Asian grays that were not blown out of the water by the Japanese and Russians prior to the whaling ban, and the Pacific gray whose recovered and no longer endangered population may rekindle the declining girdle industry.

Sei Whale

Balaenoptera borealis
One of the fastest swimmers, the Sei could be harvested only after the slower whales were seriously depleted and Honda introduced its faster four-cycle harpoon. The Sei is found in all oceans. The population count is not exact and estimates have the population at less than 50,000.

Sperm Whale

Physeter macrocephalus
The sperm whale is distinguished by the massive square head which takes up one-third of its length and is the figurehead of the Norwegian towhead community. A small reservoir in its head containing oil was once thought to hold sperm; the original name of "sperm head" was shortened by the whale's press council. A sperm whale was the arch villain in Herman Melville's classic novel, *Moby Dick.* The plot centered around the hunt for a gigantic sperm whale which consumed Captain Ahab, who was nicknamed "dick head" by the rest of the crew. The sperm whale has been hunted for centuries, principally for the spermaceti oil used in lamps and lubricants, and a waxy secretion used in perfume manufacturing called ambergris.

Blue Whale

Balaenoptera musculus
The largest mammal on earth, the blue whale can grow up to one hundred feet long and weigh up to one hundred fifty tons. Like all baleen whales, it feeds principally on krill, which is strained through the

plates in its palate. This whale's throat is only a few inches in diameter, proving that Jonah could not have been swallowed by a blue whale, another truth in parable problem.

Humpback Whale

Megaptera novaeangliae
Predictably humpbacked, this whale is distinguished by a flat head covered with knobs. While breeding, humpbacks fight rivals with major tail-lashing and bubble-blowing. The humpback is well-known for its ability to make memorable and complex songs filled with moans, groans, squeals, and other rap raptures of the deep and, with continued Asian whaling, is considering crossing over to a more popular country and western singing style.

Right Whale

Balaena glacialis
The right or black right whale is the most endangered of all the whales. With a girth almost the same as its length, this blocky critter is often identified by scaly head patches caused by whale lice, and a source of embarrassment at all-species whale reunions. The right whale was almost hunted to extinction by the mid-twentieth century as it was easy to hunt and floated once dead, allowing easy at-sea processing. Rarely sighted, the current population of right whales is left at approximately 500 mammals.

Bowhead Whale

Balaena mysticetus
A stout-bodied mature bowhead spends its entire life along the Arctic ice pack. Noticeably without a dorsal fin, the bowhead can weigh up to fifty tons and has a pronounced underbite. This whale has been so overhunted, its population now numbers less than 5,000.

Finback Whale

Balaenoptera physalus

Second in size only to the blue whale, the fast moving (twenty miles per hour) finback escaped the early slow moving whalers. Power boats introduced early in this century stopped all that and the population is thought to be stabilized around 200,000.

If you are the senior harpooner for a subsistence village in Japan, Norway, Iceland, and the former Soviet Union, a whale of a snack to feed the hungry beach blubberers is the blowhole. It's no fluke that whales have been hunted for many hundreds of years—the food byproduct tastes good. Several members of the International Whaling Commission, most notably Norway and Japan, have been taking several hundred of the thirty-foot minke whale for scientific research annually and wish to push that harvest figure up to enough whales to feed the entire Scandinavian and Asian scientific research community.

Populations that grew up on inexpensive whale meat prepare Greenpeace steaks in familiar ways. With its fine texture, aged beef color, and tenderloins that hang off both ends of your dining table, low calorie whale meat fits into any red meat recipe. If the muscles that wave at the whale watchers are too stringy, the whale of a tail is just a beaver tail (or seal flipper) on steroids and can be fixed the same way. Hold tail over heat till skin blisters. Once cool, peel skin and roast over grill.

Although nothing but fat, fresh blubber is a staple of a low cholesterol native diet. In recent tastings financed by the federal revised food group advocates, a particularly unfocused group of Native Americans showed no interest in blubber lite.

REPTILES

THE LARGEST reptiles known to man, the dinosaurs, are extinct unless you count their celluloid recreations. Public interest in the other cold-blooded vertebrates such as crocodiles, lizards, snakes, and turtles has been taken by foreign tortoises large enough for kids to ride on and domestic crocodiles large enough for kids to ride in.

The reptile census bureau hasn't been able to count all the homeless but many field biologists are privately concerned that the scales of justice are not tipped in favor of the small turtles youngsters used to net in the marsh.

American Crocodile

Crocodylus acutus
Florida, Mexico, South America, Caribbean

The saltwater version of the American alligator, the American crocodile, is identified by a more pointed snout and much sunnier disposition. A mature crocodile will grow to twelve feet long; unlike the more aggressive alligator with a long memory of the belt and handbag industry, the crocodile will shy away from humans. In Florida, these prehensile creatures feed on bass and mullet and, different from flyfishing fancy pants, do not catch, then release, tarpon. Crocodiles have been found breeding in the cooling canals of nuclear power plants and this experience may change their attitudes towards humans as a food group.

A female croc guarding her eggs from your omelet pan will question your intentions. A hatchet between the eyes sends the creature to the Big Swamp in the Sky. Boil to loosen back plates, skin and cut out white meat of the jaw, tail, and torso, and darker leg meats for use in a stew.

CROC POT STEW

Cut one pound of parboiled crocodile meat into bite-sized chunks. Chop two potatoes, four carrots, and two medium-size onions. Add all ingredients to Croc Pot or any slow cooker, adding three cups of water. Cover and let simmer for desired amount of time. Towards the end of the cooking cycle, salt and pepper to taste, adding a pinch of marjoram if desired.

Serve piping hot.

Don't cry any crocodile tears for the long lizards. The American alligator was first listed as endangered in 1967 because of the pressures of an unregulated hide industry; that protection was so successful that in 1981 the state of Florida allowed controlled hunts. In 1987, the listing for alligators changed to "threatened due to similarity of appearance" to the crocodiles, which has been called a crock by reptile rights activists.

Blunt-nosed Leopard Lizard

Gambelia silus

California

The only mainland United States lizard to be endangered, the blunt-nosed leopard lizard's round body shows a pattern of dark spots and light crossbars. The California native remains inactive underground during the winter months and, during the summer, fights developers for habitat on the sparse plains and grasslands of the San Joaquin Valley. Lizards eat insects, such as flies, bees, and grasshoppers and will supplement this regular diet with an occasional young lizard, even its own youngster, which just goes to show you that not everyone is as concerned as we are. With lizard habitat and populations shrinking, snakes, spotted skunks, and ground squirrels must hurry to take a lizard for lunch.

ROAST LIZARD

Prepare camp fire.

Skin, clean, and eviscerate lizard. Remove all interior organs and intestines, especially the poisonous lizard's gizzards.

Spit lizard and roast over camp fire until done.

This recipe is especially good for the endangered St. Croix ground lizard and the threatened Coachella Valley fringe-toed and Island night lizard. There are various recipes for the lounge lizard found all over southern California. Barbecue any gecko, iguana, or monitor lizard you find. Iguana tastes a lot like chicken, which takes a fair amount of pressure off poultry.

Plymouth Red-Bellied Turtle

Pseudemys rubriventris bangsi

Massachusetts

Living along another endangered shoreline, the small red-bellied turtles of Plymouth County, Massachusetts rest on pond bottoms in the winter and nest in the sandy soil close to the water's edge in late spring.

Turtles may be the oldest grouping of reptiles and seem safely tucked inside a hard protective shell. Raccoons still eat turtle eggs right out of the nest and largemouth bass wait for any surviving soft-shelled hatchlings to practice their breast stroke. A captive breeding program has been initiated by the Massachusetts pond pilgrims and staffed by researchers sworn to be allergic to the mighty fine tasting turtle eggs.

All turtles have arch enemies. Large domestic snapper turtles leave directional tracks to their nest omelets and sea turtles have long been a part of a healthy coyote breakfast. Humans know best how to use the entire turtle and its meat has been a staple in many diets. Warriors of the Plains Indians tribes would eat turtle steaks for its spiritual strength before doing battle; the short-living "Singa Turtles" would wear the leftover hard shell which provided little protection from army musket fire.

Serious turtle foodies feed cornmeal to their captives for a week to purge the system. To clean a turtle, chop the head off and hang the carcass to bleed. Boil for twenty minutes in salted water to loosen the shell plates and leeches and other parasites. Cool and separate

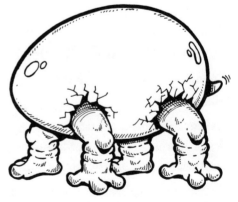

top shell from bottom. Remove and skin legs, tail, and neck and throw the rest into your favorite soups and stews.

While a bit grittier than chicken eggs and with a larger yolk, poached turtle eggs are an all-day moveable feast. To gather endangered turtle eggs, you'll have to skunk the other predators. Climb over or dig under the security fence and as soon as mom has left the nest, grab enough for breakfast. If mom is a snapper and returns before you have collected all her offspring, the yolk's on you.

POACHED TURTLE EGGS

In a small pan, add two cups of water, one pinch of salt and a teaspoon of vinegar. Set to boil.

Break turtle eggs onto a plate, no more than three at a time.

Carefully slide the eggs into the boiling water, ladling hot water over the yolks, and simmer for not more than three minutes.

Remove eggs from water and place on buttered toast. Salt and pepper to taste.

Also good for the endangered Alabama red-billed turtle and other significant sea-turtles; the olive, Kemps, Ridley, green sea, leatherback sea, and hawksbill sea turtle. The leatherback is the largest sea turtle in the world and, like your brother-in-law, has the unique ability to eliminate waste gases through its skin. It eats twice its weight daily in jellyfish and boater's plastic bags. Less than twenty-five leatherback sea turtles nest in the United States each year, out of a world population of 100,000 sexually mature females and at least one very tired male adolescent. The hawksbill turtle is cursed with an attractive shell which is the source of natural tortoiseshell that ends up as combs, fans, and other non-reptilian ornamentation. Sea turtles are listed by the Convention on International Trade in Endangered Species but Japan registered an exemption and is now the largest market for tortoiseshell products, stuffed juvenile turtles, and American cars from the 1950s with trunks full of bear gall bladders.

The tortoises have asked not to be include with the turtles, particularly the desert tortoise who is fighting for habitat unspoiled by

four-legged methane gas producers and the four-wheeled machines their mechanized cowboys ride in on. The desert tortoise is also threatened by the good folks who use them as target practice, turn them over to slow bake their bottoms, and collect them for their trophy terrariums (not to mention resort developers whose fairways are freeways cutting through the tortoise maternity wards).

San Francisco Garter Snake

Thamnophis sirtalis tetrataenia
California

This harmless, colorful snake is in trouble because of habitat destruction and its attractiveness to herpheads. Concerned herpetologists are trying to establish up to ten populations of two hundred consenting mixed adult pairs each, which in San Francisco is problematic at best.

The advantage of snakes is that there are no feathers to pluck or scales to remove. Most snake fanciers first skin their meal as it improves the taste of the snake meat ever so slightly. Run a knife edge lengthwise along the belly and undress the snake, cut off the head and throw the eyes, as snake eyes are the craps.

SNAKE ON A STAKE

Prepare camp fire.
Skin, clean, and eviscerate snake.
Spit snake and roast over camp fire until done.

This recipe can also be used for the threatened Atlantic salt marsh, Concho water, and Eastern indigo snake, but only if they threaten you first. The salt marsh snake has been a real snake-in-the-grass by cavorting with the more common *Nerodia fasciata pictiventris,* which threatens its purebred status. The large indigo snake has the particular disadvantage to be large, docile, non-poisonous, and always within reach of a big ugly stick.

CLAMS, SNAILS, CRUSTACEANS, INSECTS, ARACHNIDS, AND PLANTS

T HESE SIX LESS familiar categories are lumped, not dumped, together for easy reference. This section could easily be expanded into a separate book, and the full weight of the plant listings alone would endanger the second sailing of the Ark. It gets even more serious; the recent attention to entire ecosystems threatens the vegetarian diets of some of the super mammals. For example, the threatened cane bamboo so favored by the flyfishing purist is nothing but a flavored toothpick for giant pandas and a fair price for either is now extinct.

Clams

North America was once a good home to all freshwater mussels (commonly called clams), but now there are forty-two endangered and eight threatened bivalve mollusks.

In their life cycle, mussel larvae attach to the gills of host fish species and those that miss the passing fish, sink and die. Those who become adults eat by filtering food particles but dam impoundments, channel diversions, and sand and gravel mining have muddied the waters and clogged the clam food holes. Several clam subspecies are already beyond reproduction age with no feeling left in their love mussel. Endangered mussels are typically found in any southern states without a major league franchise and are illegally sold by hawkers outside state fish hatcheries.

SCALPED MUSSELS

Preheat oven to 325 degrees.

Remove mussels from shells and rinse in cold water. The cleaned mussels should equal one cup.

Butter casserole dish.

In a large mixing bowl, combine mussels, ½ cup of bread crumbs, and ½ cup of milk.

Pour mixture into casserole and bake until firm.

Snails

There are eight endangered and six threatened snails. These slow-moving gastropods with spiral protective shells all live in very narrow habitats, often in a single spring or stretch of river. Many of the isolated habitats are on private land so poachers move at a snail's pace under the cover of a moonless night.

SNAIL IN A PAIL

Prepare camp fire, fill medium-size pail with four cups of water and set on coals.

Remove snails from shells, scrub off slime, cut off the feet, and rinse in lightly salted water.

In boiling water, place one bouillon cube (stirring until completely dissolved), snails, and two tablespoons lightly sautéed psilocybin mushrooms. Let boil for thirty minutes.

Remove snails, drain, brush with garlic butter, and broil over remaining coals.

Relax and get solidly broiled.

Crustacaens

Shellfish of the subphylum, Crustacean, are arthropods that include amphipods, barnacles, crabs, crayfish, isopods, lobsters, and shrimp that typically have a hard outer shell, breath through gills and may move on jointed appendages.

Amphipods The only entry is the Hay's Spring amphipod living conveniently within the National Zoological Park in Washington, D.C. This listing seems like a cheap amphipod publicity trick to less successful, less politically connected zookeepers elsewhere.

Barnacles While not in any formal danger, barnacles share a little of the risk attached to the larger sea mammals.

Crabs The only threatened crab is the body crab, *Phthirius pubis,* and, while not federally protected, its vulnerability comes from all the recent attention to sexually transmitted diseases. Crabs lay their eggs, called nits, in human pubic hair, their favored habitat. The term, nit-pick, originates in the colonial custom of wives of seafaring husbands cleaning their hubby up after a hard year on the high briny. To cook body crabs, you'll need a blue ointment prescribed by your doctor, unless you have crabs large enough to be boiled or cleaned on a chopping block.

Crayfish There are three endangered crayfish; the cave, the Nashville, and the Shasta crayfish. Two smaller crayfish are of small note, except as an appetizer. Boil in salty water with a few bay leaves until red, then eat. The Nashville crayfish was listed to protect the bait-fishing source for local country and western personalities.

Isopods One of the two endangered aquatic crustaceans is found only in the water pipes of an abandoned bathhouse west of Socorro, New Mexico, and the other in the Madison Cave of Virginia. The adaptable Socorro isopod has an ancestry that began in salt water, then a freshwater lake that went dry, then upstream to a warm water spring that was finally capped for a bathhouse that has long ago

closed. These bathhouse isopods are waiting for a federal transfer to another collection point for soapy body hair, such as the co-ed black-footed ferret researcher's unisex burrow bathroom. The other isopod home, the Madison Cave, was the first cave mapped in the United States, and most famously by Thomas Jefferson who selfishly needed a place to hide his second slave family, not to mention his extra-commercial mind-altering smoking products. Both crustaceans are much too small to clean.

Lobsters A fairly-priced lobster dinner is extinct.

Shrimp There is one freshwater stream and three cave shrimp on the protected list; one of the threatened cave dwellers lives only in a sinkhole outside Gainsville, Florida. With so few Squirrel Chimney Cave shrimp left and so many sinkhole sheriffs standing guard, you'll want a recipe that is traditional, yet quick.

SHRIMP BRISQUE

Uing a can opener, remove the top from a full can of beer (Mexican if possible). Drink off ¼ of contents.

Shell, clean, and devein shrimp.

Place shrimp in beer. Using a Zippo lighter (Bic disposables also work well), heat the beer until boiling. Keep boiling until shrimp are done.

There are very few other reasons to do this to a good can of beer.

Insects

Of the twenty-three insect listings, there are seven beetles, fourteen butterflies, one token moth, and one aquatic waterbug. While pesticides and bug zappers claim their toll, collectors and other insect eaters are a major threat to American beetles. Except for the two endangered beetles coming from too-well known, too-well guarded limestone caves of Texas, the American burying beetle is so rare that descriptive locations of habitat are, to beetlemaniacs, only "New England." The two threatened tiger beetles are of high interest to collectors. The adult Puritan tiger beetle imitates its nemesis, the human waterfront real estate prospect; tiger beetles feed and mate on the beach, then use the cliff areas to build nests and deposit their eggs. The other two threatened beetles live in shrinking California wetlands.

The most prevalent beach beetle is not threatened yet, but is in constant danger due to the shortage of good Volkswagen mechanics.

Insects have a high nutritional value and are stuffed full of protein. Stripped of their outer hardware, the exposed soft bodies of beetles can be fried in oil, boiled, steamed, or roasted over an open fire.

BEETLE BROCHETTE

Prepare camp fire or preheat oven with rotisserie to 375 degrees.

Shell and clean twelve beetles.

Cut two small onions, two red bell peppers, and three large mushrooms into quarters.

Using metal skewers, alternate beetles and vegetables.

Drizzle olive oil over packed skewers and roast in either an oven or over an open fire until done.

Serve on a bed of wild rice.

Once you have the taste for soft underbellies, move on to the larvae of butterflies. Change the diet and taste of the larvae by running cornmeal through their alimentary canal for a week and use any preparation listed above. No shelling required.

Butterflies

The eleven endangered and three threatened butterflies find the going the roughest in the Golden State. Seven of the endangered butterflies live in California, including the possibly extinct Palos Verdes blue butterfly and the rarest mission blue butterfly. Habitat destruction threaten all the butterfly habitats; the preferred habitat of Lange's metalmark butterfly was so beaten down by concerned whalewatch-

ers over the plight of Humphrey the humpbacked whale stuck in the Sacramento River that now unescorted groups have to leave their Birkenstocks at the gate. Pesticides used to control other airborne pests such as mosquitoes have endangered the Schaus swallowtail, a tropical Keys butterfly.

Collectors threaten all butterflies and the Safari Club is being petitioned by its butterfly collector members to add a new trophy category called "The Grand Squash."

The rare North American sphinx moth has been laying its eggs on the wrong plant and its larvae are starving. Whoops. The Ask Meadow naucorid, a threatened little waterbug native to Nevada, is just glad to be part of the larger gambling picture.

Arachnids

The arachnid family includes spiders, scorpions, mites, and ticks. The only three federally protected entries are under one-third inch long. The Tooth Cave spider, Tooth Cave Pseudoscorpion, and Bee Creek Cave Harvestman all live in the limestone caves edging the suburban explosion of Austin, Texas. If three arachnids aren't enough to stop the urban sprawl, the endangered Tooth Cave ground beetle will file as an insect of the court. "Ditto!" squawks the endangered black-capped vireo nesting nearby, who has forsworn eating any of the above until the caves are placed off-limits to busybody protectionists. Mites and ticks, particularly the deer tick that carries Lymes disease, are doing well, what with all the loose American skin to hide in.

Plants

Almost half of the protected listings are plants but this large grouping receives few of any recovery dollars. Perennials, shrubs, mints, annuals, ferns, trees, and thistle all have been interviewed by plant speech therapists and they aren't going to take much more of this.

Plant life is less than idyllic. In addition to general habitat degradation and destruction, interior decorators are moving the outdoors indoors, creating exotic plant-filled terrariums and rooms and rock garden collections. Cactus plants and the other succulents that make up over ten percent of the endangered list reproduce slower than the collectors who steal them. The honest and thoughtful aquarium suppliers group that has done so much good to fragile coral reef and tropical fish populations have expanded their inventory for human hot houses and promise to introduce kelp beds for toilets.

Mammal bullies are another problem. The endangered *hedyotis degeneri* of Oahu is a shrub that shares habitat with rooting feral pigs; these pigs open the ground to invasive species carried in the pigs feces, such as the dreaded ca-ca plant. The feral goats of Kauai eat the Na Pali beach hedyotis shrubs frantically trying to grow up the slopes to shrub safety. Other limited range plants are in similar danger. The Sentry milk-vetch, a perennial that only grows on the south rim of the Grand Canyon National Park, is trampled by hikers and gawkers. Roadkill victims, such as the rare endangered lily Harper's Beauty, have the misfortune to grow along well-traveled visitor routes.

The listings must be incomplete. There are no protected plants in South Dakota (or in Washington State, but the mountain goats of the Olympic National Park aren't talking) and only one fern is protected in Alaska; commercial low-flying sport-harvesting flights are available to "harvest" these ferns from the air.

Vegetarians are the biggest threat to rare and endangered plants. Prohibited by social custom from eating their neighbor's shrubs and indoor decorative plants, over-active herbivores are hiking, climbing, and four-wheeling to the free flora feedlots. The only risk is the consumption of roadside grasses that have been sprayed by highway crews and domestic pets. Vegetarian pain-in-the-butts claim that the combination of a short food fast with a meatless diet reduces the aching associated with hemorrhoidal arthritis.

Most plants can be eaten if pre-chewed by a hiking partner or senior chaperone. Several other rules of caution:

- Watch what other mammals eat and successfully keep down.
- If awful tasting, avoid anyway, no matter what essential food group assigned by the camp fire survivalist Nazi.
- Eat only the berries that you know, excluding dingleberries.
- Boil all roots and tubers, but not in the same pot with socks.
- Avoid eating any mushrooms that you haven't smoked before.
- Avoid eating any fungus in your shorts unless as a last resort.
- Eat only the moss growing on the north side of your spouse.

When preparing plants, boil them until tender and skim poisons off top of water. Branches and shrubs take longer. If larger twigs and pine cones aren't cooked until soft, your evening toilet will be very difficult.

MAJOR FORMER ENDANGERED SPECIES

THE UNITED STATES Fish and Wildlife Service reports to Congress on the status of the threatened and endangered species using recovery categories of improving, stable, unknown, declining, or extinct. The report on the following familiar sampling is a combination of the above.

Giant Ground Sloth

Evolving into a more human form known as the giant couch sloth, this mammal is usually related to you by birth or marriage. Able to create and survive in a deteriorating habitat, poor breeding habits threaten the survival of this crossbred subspecies.

Great Auk

Last seen in 1844 by a witness who is also extinct.

Carolina Parakeet

The only member of the true parrot family that lived and bred in the United States. This gregarious colorful parrot was shot by colonial landowners, plucked for hats, and poached by the pet trade. The last known North American parrot died in 1914.

Dodo

This flightless bird became extinct in the early 1860s but remnant subgroup migrations are sighted along major political flyways every four years.

Passenger Pigeon

The most abundant bird in America in the first half of the nineteeth century, flocks of passenger pigeons could block the sun for hours.

These pigeons were once thought (as early abacuses couldn't count that high) to number as many as fifteen billion. Martha, the last passenger pigeon, died unnoticed in the Cincinnati Zoo in 1914, which still doesn't explain why the sun is rarely visible in the Pacific Northwest.

Tasmanian Wolf

A Tasmanian wolf is a marsupial with a head of a wolf that walks like a tiger, or used to walk like a tiger. The wolf was painted as a sheep killer in the late nineteenth century and thought extinct by watchful, gun-toting sheep ranchers. Possible recent sightings by the Tasmanian Quaffers Society wolfing down the local brew have caused the ranchers to lock and load.

MAJOR NON-U.S. ENDANGERED SPECIES

To CONTROL the race to taste the exotic, wear the erotic, or to simply cover the last open space on a trophy wall, the Convention on International Trade in Endangered Species was created and signed by 119 countries to restrict or stop the importation of threatened or endangered species from countries whose white colonial idea of big game management is to surround elephant herds with native villages.

Asian Elephant

With an estimated population of 40,000, one-tenth the number of the merely threatened African elephants, this endangered pachyderm eats its way out of house and home. An appetite that requires up to 500 pounds of vegetables every day does not engender support from local village truck farmers. Exploding human populations, not guns, keep the Asian elephant in check, and its habitat checkered. Once free-ranging all over Asia, the elephant is now found only in India, Sri Lanka, and southeast Asia, hard at work pulling old-growth exotic hardwoods and disabled Land Rovers.

Black Rhinoceros

With the rhinoceros's habitat pushed back by agricultural development and poached for its horn, this African's numbers have dropped by sixty-five percent during past ten years to five thousand. The two horns of the black rhino are worth up to $20,000 each on the black market and used to fashion the most prized dagger handles for Arabs going through manly rites of passage or ground up into love potions for Asian clerics. Wildlife officials in Zimbabwe and Namibia are cutting the horns off their shrinking populations with chainsaws and, except for a little lightheadedness and buzzing in the ears, the rhino's self-esteem remains intact. Rhinoplasty is available for those individuals whose nose is seriously out of joint.

Giant Panda

With as few as one thousand left in the wild, these black and white mammals live in remote mountain areas in China. These gentle creatures ever so slowly pack away twenty to sixty pounds of hard-to-digest young bamboo shoots daily and spend the warm afternoons posing for wildlife artists. Once hunted for its coat to make sleeping mats that unfortunately had the folk tradition of keeping evil spirits away, the giant panda is defended against poaching with a death penalty, but has no protection from Chinese officials either selling or renting pandas to the highest bidder looking to rebuild zoo gate receipts. The success of reproduction of the over one hundred captive pandas has not been remarkable, particularly at Deng Xia Ping's PandaLand where at 2:00 PM, 4:00 PM, and sometimes at 6:00 PM, shy giant pandas are expected to perform sex acts on bamboo beds for vacationing Taiwanese families. With the small energy reserves produced from all that bamboo, giant pandas avoid conflict, don't chase small animals no matter how tasty, and would rather mate by proxy than wait for both to be in season.

The Asiatic black bear is under intense pressure from the Asian need for gall bladders, which have the reputation to cure many human ailments. The Chinese have the gall to farm for the secretion and promise to stop only when they are cut in on the cuddly panda bear toy royalties.

There are no endangered bears in the United States but the grizzly threatens to make horribilus hash out of slow moving wildlife watchers, making amateur photographers without a zoom lens an endangered species. The Louisiana black bear, the original Teddy bear (named after the one pardoned by the great white presidential hunter while on a political junket) numbers less than one hundred and its publicly protected tree homes on privately owned timberland are being threatened. The polar bear or Eskimo "Nanook" is protected by the Marine Animal Protection Act of 1972 and the large carnivore will do well as long as the native sled dogs aren't replaced by snowmobiles.

Bear meat enthusiasts are quick to point out that the bear should be real dead before you start carving on its hindquarters, or Smokey will return the favor. Old-timers are split right down the camp fire as to whether a lean spring bear is better eating than a fat fall bruin slipped into its pajamas for a long winter's nap. While fat can make most meat sweeter, bear fat is strong and, except for a few old lard-buckets who disagree, should be removed and discarded. The most generous bear eaters will say bear meat tastes a lot like pork but then

again, it can't taste like an eight hundred pound chicken. Like pork, the danger of trichinosis is present. Unless you want to freeze the meat for a month, most recipes include a long, hot bake.

With international sleight-of-hand, the bull-ish Asian bear market and trade in bear paws has the prosthetic industry work-ing overtime. The paws of spring bears that have healed from the cave dig-ging in the fall supply a recipe handed down from generation to generation.

PAW'S BEAR PAW

Preheat oven to 350 degrees.

Skin and clean paw.

In a shallow dish combine ½ cup flour, salt and pepper, and a pinch of cayenne pepper. Mix well and dredge paw in this mixture.

Heat either bacon or bear fat in open skillet and brown paw.

Arrange bear paw in casserole dish with potatoes, carrots, and onions. Add one cup of water and lay four to six strips of bacon across the top.

Bake for three to four hours.

Serve in the familiar hand-to-mouth movement.

Mountain Gorilla

Threatened by deforestation, poaching, and the fatty diet served by Hollywood crew caterers, there are fewer than five hundred mountain gorillas picking their butts along the Rwanda-Zaire-Uganda border. Studies of the great apes have yielded sympathy and empathy with human similarities; visitors to the high mountain research camps can't help but notice how much these large primates remind them of their last employer. The male alpha gorillas command a harem which, in these troubled yet enlightened times, have to be fleshed out with white female biologists from the United States and European universities.

Snow Leopard

Hiding not high enough in the mountains of Central Asia, these big cats have been hunted for their skin and to protect livestock feeding above the treeline. There are less than 5,000 snow leopards left and the remaining adults want to move to Las Vegas to entertain overfed, drunk tour groups in big glitzy hotels. At home, snow leopards eat mountain goats, deer, marmots, and sleeping sherpas. While few humans shoot leopards for food, there aren't many cat parts that an Asian pharmacist won't use: eyes, bones, whiskers, and even the scream may have commercial value. The Siberian tiger shares the same predatory pharmaceutical attention and has even less protection since the breakup of the Soviet Union. Without a steady diet of political prisoners from the Siberian gulags, the tiger is expected to turn on the wealthy former party apparatchiks retiring in the newly developed resort archipelagos on their dead seas.

AFTERWORD

A NIMALS and plants that can or will adapt to a changing environment are the ones most likely to survive. So the Everglade kite, an endangered hawk that only eats the apple snail and refuses government-grown broccoli as a diet replacement, better be concerned with apple snail habitat. If and when the last elephant bites the dust, what will the dung beetle do? If the Seattle gadabout drinks only latte grande, what happens when mocha grande overtakes their historic latte-sipping habitat?

What is not needed is another federal entitlement program with inalienable rights to suitable woodpecker habitat, without considering suitable habitat for others in the pecking order. Of the thirteen hundred listed species, over three hundred of the eight hundred United States entries have approved recovery plans. Mammals, birds, and plants are doing best but the status of the invertebrates is uncertain. Freshwater mussels are mostly in decline.

All is not lost. A once thought extinct species such as the Madagascar puchard, a fresh water duck, has been re-discovered and an all-new species, the black-faced lion tamarin, was recently found near São Paulo, Brazil (although with remarkable facial similarities to the pioneering tamarin recovery team leader).

The competition for suitable habitat quickens. Over the last thirty-five years, world population has almost doubled from 2.6 billion to 5 billion happy campers. By 2100, this count is expected to jump to 10 billion caring, sharing people and this cookbook will then be updated and offered as an international multi-volume set.

ABOUT THE AUTHOR

Master guide to all-that-is-wild-in-the-outdoors and director of a famous nature study correspondence course, "Buck" Peterson has been keeping his own endangered species count and is understandably concerned that his totals don't jibe with the federal and state numbers. He's called the Department of the Interior and the Fish and Wildlife Service offices several times but has been unable to get anyone to return his calls.

"Buck" did receive a call from the White House and has taken a temporary, yet important, position as caretaker of the Serendipity Spotted Owl Sanctuary in a privately owned fourth growth tree farm in the Pacific Northwest. Asked recently how, in general, it's all going, "Buck" assured the local birdwatcher chapter that "All things considered, as good as can be expected."